# JAMES BLUNT

# ECHOES OF LIFE
# AND MELODY

## AMANDA GERALDINE

# TABLE OF CONTENTS

## PREFACE

James Blunt, originally known as James Hillier Blount, was born on February 22, 1974. He is an accomplished English singer, songwriter, and musician whose journey in the entertainment industry is as fascinating as his music itself. However, Blunt's story begins even before his musical career took off.

Before becoming a renowned artist, James Blunt led a different life. He served as a reconnaissance officer in the Life Guards regiment of the British Army. His commitment to duty led him to serve under NATO during the intense Kosovo War of 1999, showcasing his dedication to a cause larger than himself.

After his honorable service in the military, Blunt transitioned into the world of music, captivating audiences worldwide. His defining moment came in

2004 with the launch of his debut album, "Back to Bedlam." This marked the beginning of his meteoric rise to fame, a journey that would forever change the music industry.

The album's standout tracks, "You're Beautiful" and "Goodbye My Lover," resonated deeply with listeners, propelling Blunt into the international spotlight. "You're Beautiful" not only reached the top spot on music charts in the UK and the US but also dominated numerous other countries, becoming a global sensation.

"Back to Bedlam" wasn't just an album; it was a phenomenon. With sales exceeding a staggering 11 million copies worldwide, the album not only dominated the UK Albums Chart but also achieved a remarkable number two position in the US. Its monumental success established it as the best-selling album of the 2000s in the UK and secured a permanent place in the annals of UK chart history.

James Blunt's impact on the music industry is immeasurable, with over 20 million records sold worldwide. His exceptional talent has been recognized through various prestigious awards, including two Brit Awards, where he was crowned Best British Male in 2006. Blunt's artistic prowess also earned him two MTV Video Music Awards and two Ivor Novello Awards, further solidifying his status as a musical virtuoso.

Blunt's achievements transcend music, as he garnered significant attention in other realms as well. His remarkable contributions led to five Grammy Award nominations, a testament to his versatility and creativity. In 2016, the University of Bristol acknowledged his immense influence on the world of music by awarding him an Honorary Doctorate of Music.

In conclusion, James Blunt's journey from being a dedicated reconnaissance officer to becoming a global music sensation is a testament to his unwavering commitment, artistic brilliance, and profound impact on the world. His narrative encompasses courage, dedication, and the power of music to transcend boundaries and touch the hearts of millions.

# EARLY YEARS

Born on February 22, 1974, James Blount entered the world as James Hillier Blount at Tidworth Camp military hospital in Hampshire. He was the eldest of three siblings born to Jane Ann Farran (née Amos) and Colonel Charles Blount. The roots of his family's legacy trace back to their Danish ancestors' arrival in England during the 10th century.

Blount's upbringing was marked by the dynamic lifestyle of a military family. While his mother initiated a ski chalet company in the French Alpine resort of Méribel, his father embarked on a multifaceted military career. Starting as a cavalry officer in the 13th/18th Royal Hussars, his father eventually transitioned into becoming a helicopter pilot, eventually rising to the esteemed rank of Colonel in the Army Air Corps. This lineage of military service resonated deeply with Blount's upbringing.

Growing up primarily in St Mary Bourne, Hampshire, Blount's childhood was characterized by frequent relocations. He moved every two years, a rhythm dictated by his father's military assignments across England, including Middle Wallop, Netheravon, and York. Additionally, his family's journey took them to Cyprus (Nicosia) and Germany (Soest). The family's connection to diverse locations was further exemplified by their ownership of the Cley Windmill in Cley-next-the-Sea.

Education played a crucial role in shaping Blount's path. He attended Elstree School in Woolhampton and later continued his studies at Harrow School in Middlesex. Here, he excelled academically, achieving A-levels in physics, chemistry, and economics. His insatiable curiosity led him to the

University of Bristol, where he pursued a dual degree in aerospace manufacturing engineering and sociology. This academic journey culminated in his graduation in 1996 with a BSc (Hons) degree.

Blount's connection to his alma mater remained strong even years later, as evidenced by the radio broadcast titled 'James Blunt: From A to Z,' which aired on Burst Radio in March 2022. His diverse interests extended beyond academics, mirroring his father's passions. Like his father, Blount is an accomplished pilot, earning his fixed-winged private pilot license at the remarkable age of 16. Alongside his aviation pursuits, he fostered a deep fascination with motorbikes during this phase of his life.

In retrospect, James Blount's early life laid the foundation for his multifaceted career and diverse talents. The amalgamation of military heritage, exposure to various cultures, and a commitment to education and exploration all contributed to shaping the remarkable artist and individual he would become.

# MILITARY YEARS

James Blunt's journey took a compelling turn as he delved into a committed phase of military service. Having secured an army bursary for his university education, Blunt was honor-bound to dedicate a minimum of four years to the armed forces. His path led him to the prestigious Royal Military Academy, Sandhurst, where he underwent rigorous training as part of intake 963. Following this, he received his commission into the Life Guards, a revered reconnaissance regiment, rising through the ranks to attain the position of captain.

Blunt's service with the Life Guards brought him to Combermere Barracks, where the regiment was primarily stationed. His training took him across borders, including a significant stint in Alberta, Canada, as part of the British Army Training Unit Suffield. The unit's deployment to Canada in 1998

11

was instrumental in honing their combat skills, as they played the opposing force in intensive training exercises.

However, Blunt's most impactful military assignment arrived in 1999 when he volunteered for a crucial mission. Joining a Blues and Royals squadron, he was deployed to Kosovo as part of NATO's peacekeeping efforts. Tasked with reconnaissance along the North Macedonia–Yugoslavia border, Blunt's troop operated ahead of the front lines, identifying and targeting Serbian forces to support NATO's bombing campaign.

A pivotal moment occurred on June 12, 1999, when Blunt's troop led a formidable NATO peacekeeping force toward Pristina International Airport from the North Macedonia border. The situation grew tense as a Russian military contingent had already taken control of the airport before their arrival.

Amid escalating tensions, American NATO commander Wesley Clark issued an order for the airport to be forcibly taken from the Russians. In a stand that reverberated with resolute integrity, British commander General Mike Jackson refused to comply, conveying that they wouldn't instigate a world war for such a cause. Blunt's perspective aligns with General Jackson's decision, emphasizing that he too would have declined the order if not for the general's intervention.

Amid the intense duties of his Kosovo assignment, Blunt found solace and expression through music. He carried his guitar affixed to the outside of his tank and would occasionally perform for locals and fellow troops. It was during this period that he penned the poignant song "No Bravery," encapsulating the complex emotions and experiences he witnessed.

Blunt's unwavering commitment extended beyond Kosovo, as he continued his military service in various capacities. In November 2000, he transitioned to the Household Cavalry Mounted Regiment in London, where he contributed to the Queen's Guard. His diverse experiences led him to unexpected opportunities, such as his appearance on the television program "Girls on Top," which showcased individuals with unconventional career paths.

His military service also saw him participating in poignant moments of history. He stood guard at the coffin of Queen Mother Elizabeth Bowes-Lyon during her lying-in-state ceremony and was a part of the solemn funeral procession on April 9, 2002.

Even amidst his military engagements, Blunt's love for skiing shone through. He captained the Household Cavalry alpine ski team in Verbier, Switzerland, achieving the esteemed title of the

Royal Armoured Corps giant slalom champion in 2000.

After a six-year journey within the military, Blunt concluded his service on October 1, 2002. This chapter of his life was marked by duty, integrity, and experiences that would shape his artistic endeavors and worldview for years to come.

# MUSIC CAREER

## EARLY CAREER

James Blunt's musical journey began as a child, with lessons in piano and violin. However, it was the introduction to the electric guitar at the age of 14, thanks to a fellow student at Harrow, that ignited his passion for creating music. Even during his academic pursuits at Bristol University, his inclination towards the music industry was evident. His dissertation titled "The Commodification of Image – Production of a Pop Idol" delved into the dynamics of pop culture. Notably, sociologist and rock critic Simon Frith, a prominent figure in the Mercury Music Prize, played a role in shaping Blunt's academic exploration.

While balancing his duties in the army, Blunt utilized his downtime to craft songs. A pivotal moment arose when a backing vocalist and collaborator suggested he reach out to Todd Interland, manager of Elton John. Interland's interest was piqued when he listened to Blunt's demo, particularly captivated by the track "Goodbye My Lover." This led to a crucial meeting that set the wheels in motion for Blunt's musical aspirations.

With a decision to pursue music more seriously, Blunt left the British Army in 2002, marking a pivotal transition in his life. He adopted the stage name "James Blunt," a choice influenced in part by its ease of spelling and pronunciation. This decision also provided a distinct separation between his musical identity and his legal last name, "Blount."

Navigating the industry proved challenging, with record contracts remaining elusive. Executives raised concerns about his posh speaking voice, reflecting the socio-economic divisions of Britain.

However, fate took a positive turn when Linda Perry, who was in the process of launching her label Custard Records, stumbled upon Blunt's promotional tape during a London visit. Hearing him perform live at the South by Southwest Music Festival solidified her interest, leading her to extend an offer that very night. Within a short span, Blunt signed a recording contract with her.

The journey led him across the Atlantic to Los Angeles, where he met with producer Tom Rothrock. This encounter marked a significant step forward in shaping Blunt's musical direction.

In essence, James Blunt's early music career was a convergence of talent, serendipitous encounters, and a relentless pursuit of artistic expression. From his formative experiences with instruments to his academic exploration of pop culture, every facet of his journey culminated in the decision to embrace music wholeheartedly, setting the stage for the impactful musical legacy he would go on to create.

# BACK TO BEDLAM (2003-2006)

In 2003, Blunt embarked on the recording of his debut album, "Back to Bedlam," under the production of Tom Rothrock. The recording sessions took place in Conway Recording Studios and Rothrock's own home studio in Los Angeles. Blunt showcased his musical versatility by playing multiple instruments himself throughout the album. Interestingly, during this period, he found lodging with the esteemed actress Carrie Fisher. Notably, Fisher's creative input extended to naming the album, and an unconventional recording location: Blunt recorded the song "Goodbye My Lover" in her bathroom. The culmination of these efforts led to the release of "Back to Bedlam" in the UK in October 2004.

Blunt's musical journey began to gain traction with his debut single in the UK, "High." Co-written with Ricky Ross of Deacon Blue, the song initially found itself below the Top 100 of the UK Singles Chart. However, as the subsequent hit "You're Beautiful" gained momentum, "High" experienced a resurgence and reached the Top 75 after being re-released. The song's popularity extended beyond UK borders, as it was selected for a Vodafone commercial in Italy and achieved Top 10 status in that country.

While Blunt's debut album initially flew under the radar of major UK music journals, his live performances, often in support of more established artists, received generally positive feedback. Reviewers noted his lack of extensive performing experience and occasional inconsistency in engaging with audiences. His musical style was likened to the works of artists like Damien Rice and David Gray.

March 2004 marked a significant moment as Blunt performed in support of Katie Melua in Manchester. Alex McCann of Designer Magazine predicted Blunt's imminent rise to prominence, foreseeing future accomplishments such as a number one album, a Brit Award, and numerous accolades.

Following the album's release, Blunt's trajectory continued to ascend. He secured coveted concert support slots for prominent musicians like Elton John and Lloyd Cole and the Commotions in late 2004 and early 2005. Additionally, Blunt and his band found a residency at London's renowned club, 93 Feet East, solidifying their presence in the music scene.

In March 2005, Blunt released his second single, "Wisemen," further cementing his place in the industry and setting the stage for the remarkable career that was about to unfold.

James Blunt's musical career experienced a seismic shift with the release of his third single, "You're Beautiful." This song proved to be his breakout hit, making a significant impact on both sides of the Atlantic.

Upon its debut, "You're Beautiful" entered the UK charts at number 12. However, its popularity soared, propelling it to the coveted number one spot just six weeks later. The song received extensive airplay in the UK, contributing to the ascent of his album "Back to Bedlam" to the top of the UK Albums Chart. This remarkable achievement earned Blunt and his co-writers the prestigious Ivor Novello Award for Most Performed Work.

The resonance of "You're Beautiful" wasn't limited to the UK. It swiftly crossed over to mainland Europe, emerging as one of the defining hits of the summer in 2005 across the continent. In the US, the song took an unconventional path, debuting on the airwaves of WPLJ, a prominent New York City radio station, even before its official release to radio. Once released, the song climbed into the Top 10 across three radio formats: Adult Contemporary Music, Hot Adult Top 40 Tracks, and Adult Album Alternative.

Blunt's impact on the American music scene was monumental. He became the first British artist in almost a decade to top the Billboard Hot 100 when "You're Beautiful" claimed the number one spot in 2006. The previous British artist to achieve this feat had been Elton John in 1997 with "Candle in the Wind 1997."

Following the momentum of "You're Beautiful," Blunt's other tracks gained traction as well. "Goodbye My Lover" was released as the fourth single in the UK in December 2005, and it became the second single in the US. Both "High" and "Wisemen" were re-released in 2006, contributing to the continued success of "Back to Bedlam."

Blunt's accolades continued to pour in, with five Brit Award nominations in 2006. He secured victories in the Best British Male Solo Artist and Best Pop Act categories, all while embarking on an extensive 11-month world tour. His impact was also felt on the international stage, as he received two awards at the 2006 MTV Video Music Awards, including Best Male Video for "You're Beautiful."

Blunt's prominence led to appearances on notable platforms such as The Oprah Winfrey Show and Saturday Night Live. His album's tracks found their way into television shows, films, and advertising campaigns, enhancing his visibility even further.

The commercial success of "Back to Bedlam" was nothing short of remarkable. The album sold an astonishing 11.2 million copies worldwide and topped album charts in 16 countries. In the US alone, it sold 2.6 million copies and achieved a 2× platinum certification. In his native Britain, the album surpassed three million sales, earning a remarkable 10× platinum certification and securing a spot in the Guinness Book of World Records for the fastest-selling album in a single year. Blunt's musical journey had transformed him from an unknown artist to a global sensation, leaving an indelible mark on the music industry.

In 2005, James Blunt was a force to be reckoned with on the live music scene, performing a staggering 90 live shows primarily in the UK and Europe. His talent also earned him a spot supporting Jason Mraz on a North American tour. Kicking off in January 2006, the "Back to Bedlam World Tour" traversed through cities in Europe, the UK, Australia, New Zealand, and Japan. The tour's extensive itinerary included three separate headline tours across North America, culminating in November of the same year. Remarkably, excluding promotional events, Blunt managed to perform over 140 live shows in 2006 alone.

Blunt's music videos from the "Back To Bedlam" era carried a consistent theme of symbolism and dark imagery. Each video was meticulously crafted to convey a narrative that went beyond the music itself. In the video for "High," he was buried in a desert, while the first iteration of the "Wisemen" video depicted him as a kidnapped hostage. "You're Beautiful" alluded to a darker theme with imagery of suicide as he leapt off a cliff into the sea. The video for "Goodbye My Lover" portrayed Blunt as an outsider in a love triangle, visualizing the couple's interactions. Symbolism continued in the re-release videos, with "High" featuring Blunt running through a forest and "Wisemen" showcasing him burning identification papers while engulfed in flames.

Blunt's artistic versatility extended beyond music videos. His appearance on an episode of Sesame Street in November 2007, where he sang about triangles to the melody of "You're Beautiful," showcased his ability to engage with diverse audiences. A humorous twist came when parody artist Weird Al Yankovic created a version of "You're Beautiful" titled "You're Pitiful." Although Blunt personally approved the parody, his label Atlantic Records intervened, preventing its commercial release. Despite this, Weird Al made the song available for free download on his website.

In a testament to his enduring impact, Blunt's debut album "Back to Bedlam" achieved a remarkable milestone. On December 28, 2009, BBC Radio 1 announced that the album was the biggest-selling album of the 2000s decade in the United Kingdom. This accolade solidified Blunt's place in music history as a trailblazer and a true musical phenomenon.

# ALL THE LOST SOULS (2007-2008)

James Blunt's second studio album, "All the Lost Souls," marked another significant chapter in his music career. Released on September 17, 2007, in the UK and a day later in North America, the album made an impressive debut by selling 65,000 units in its first week. Astonishingly, it attained gold certification in the UK within just four days of release. By January 2008, the album's sales reached 600,000 copies in the UK and a remarkable 4.5 million copies globally.

The genesis of "All the Lost Souls" took place at Blunt's home in Ibiza during the winter of 2006-2007. Five of the album's ten tracks had been performed during his previous tours, but they underwent refinement in lyrics, melodies, and harmonies for the studio recording. The album benefited from the expertise of Blunt's touring band and producer Tom Rothrock.

While Blunt's debut album initially garnered limited critical attention, his sophomore effort drew widespread commentary from major music publications and newspapers around the world. Reviews for "All the Lost Souls" varied from mixed to positive, earning a 53/100 rating on Metacritic. While some critics were less enthusiastic, others acknowledged Blunt's growth as an artist. Liz Hoggard of The Observer praised his "troubadour yearning" that was impossible to resist.

The album's first single, "1973," was inspired by Blunt's experiences at Pacha, an Ibiza club that opened in that year. The song became a hit, reaching number one on the Billboard European Hot 100 Singles chart. The second single, "Same Mistake," was released in December 2007 but had a lukewarm performance on the UK charts. However, it gained traction in South American countries, including reaching number one in Brazil. The third single, "Carry You Home," reinvigorated the album's success, peaking at number 20 on the UK charts and propelling the album back into the Top 10.

During this album cycle, Blunt engaged in notable collaborations. He worked with French rapper Sinik on the song "Je Réalise," which incorporated elements from Blunt's track "I'll Take Everything." He also recorded a duet with Laura Pausini titled "Primavera in anticipo," which contributed to her album's success in Italy.

Blunt's dedication to his music was reflected in his relentless touring schedule. He embarked on his second world tour in 2007 and 2008, including a performance at London's O2 Arena. He also supported Sheryl Crow on a tour alongside Toots and the Maytals in 2008.

The album's legacy continued with a re-release on November 24, 2008, as a deluxe edition. This edition featured new album artwork, a new single titled "Love, Love, Love," and the documentary "James Blunt: Return to Kosovo." Blunt's second studio album further solidified his place in the music industry and showcased his evolution as an artist.

# SOME KIND OF TROUBLE (2010-2013)

James Blunt's third studio album, titled "Some Kind of Trouble," marked another phase of his musical journey. Released on November 8, 2010, the album entered the UK charts at number four, with an impressive 100,000 copies sold within its debut week. The album's lead single, "Stay the Night," was released on October 27, 2010. While the single enjoyed better success in Europe, reaching number two on the European Airplay Chart for five consecutive weeks, its performance on the UK charts was less prominent, reaching number 37 in the top 40.

The second single from the album, "So Far Gone," was released in the UK on January 3, 2011. Subsequently, the third single, "If Time Is All I Have," hit the UK market on April 4, 2011. The critical reception to "Some Kind of Trouble" was mixed, with opinions varying among reviewers.

Allmusic provided a positive assessment, noting that the album represented a step in the right direction for Blunt, showcasing a move toward sincere love songs free from pretension. In contrast, BBC Music's review suggested that while the album wasn't terrible, it lacked a clear sense of advancement and questioned its potential impact on Blunt's overall career trajectory.

In terms of commercial success, the album achieved worldwide sales of over one million copies as of February 2011. The album's release marked another chapter in James Blunt's artistic evolution, demonstrating his commitment to exploring new musical directions while maintaining his signature heartfelt style.

# MOON LANDING (2013-2017)

James Blunt's fourth album, "Moon Landing," emerged on the music scene on October 18, 2013. The album reunited Blunt with producer Tom Rothrock, known for their work together on "Back to Bedlam." The album's lead single, "Bonfire Heart," made a notable entrance by debuting at number six and later climbing to number four on the UK Singles Chart. However, its impact extended well beyond the UK, reaching number one in countries like Australia, Germany, Switzerland, and Austria, and securing a place in the top 10 in various other nations.

A significant development occurred on September 16, 2014, as Blunt took to his official Instagram account to announce a re-release of "Moon Landing." This enhanced version, titled "Moon Landing – Apollo Edition," was set to hit the shelves on November 3, 2014. The expanded edition boasted a total of 19 tracks, including the 11 original tracks from the album, three bonus tracks from the deluxe version ("Telephone," "Kiss This Love Goodbye," and "Hollywood"), and five brand-new tracks ("Smoke Signals," "When I Find Love Again," "Breathe," "Trail of Broken Hearts," and "Working it Out"). On the same day as the announcement, the new track "When I Find Love Again" premiered on BBC's Radio 2, followed by the release of its official music video on October 14, 2014.

The re-released "Moon Landing - Apollo Edition" also featured a live DVD containing a recording of Blunt's performance during the 2014 edition of the Paléo Festival in Switzerland. The inclusion of this live performance added an extra layer of richness to the album's expanded edition.

Expanding his horizons beyond music, Blunt made an intriguing career move. On May 3, 2015, he was confirmed as a replacement for Ronan Keating on the seventh season of The X Factor Australia. He took on the role of a judge, alongside American rock musician Chris Isaak and returning judges Guy Sebastian and Dannii Minogue. This venture allowed Blunt to showcase his expertise and provide guidance to aspiring musical talents.

With "Moon Landing" and its subsequent expanded edition, James Blunt continued to captivate audiences with his evocative melodies and heartfelt lyrics, further solidifying his place in the world of music and entertainment.

# THE AFTERLOVE AND WALK AWAY (2017-2019)

In the beginning of 2016, Blunt shared exciting news through his newsletter that he had embarked on the creation of his fifth album. This forthcoming album was aptly named "The Afterlove." Building anticipation, the album was eventually released in March 2017. This release marked another chapter in Blunt's discography, offering fans new music that continued to showcase his signature emotional depth and musical versatility.

In 2019, Blunt ventured into a collaboration that showcased his willingness to explore different genres. He joined forces with German DJ and producer Alle Farben to bring forth the dance music track titled "Walk Away." This collaboration was a departure from Blunt's usual style, demonstrating his openness to experimenting with diverse musical sounds and styles.

The years 2017 to 2019 highlighted Blunt's dedication to his craft and his willingness to evolve as an artist. "The Afterlove" album and the collaboration on "Walk Away" showcased his ability to adapt to changing musical landscapes while remaining true to his artistic essence.

# ONCE UPON A MIND AND WHO WE USED TO BE (2019-2023)

In October 2019, Blunt unveiled his sixth studio album, titled "Once Upon a Mind." This album showcased his continued commitment to crafting emotive and introspective music. The lead single from the album, "Cold," was released on August 29, 2019, building anticipation for the full album release.

In November 2021, Blunt unveiled his first "greatest hits" album titled "The Stars Beneath My Feet (2004-2021)." This compilation featured his most celebrated tracks from his career, spanning the years 2004 to 2021. Notably, the album also included four new songs, demonstrating Blunt's ongoing creativity and dedication to his craft. Among these new tracks, "Love Under Pressure" and "Unstoppable" were released as singles, resonating with fans old and new. To accompany the album,

Blunt embarked on a Greatest Hits tour, treating his audience to his iconic tracks in live performances.

Continuing his musical journey, Blunt had exciting news to share in 2023. On August 2, he revealed his forthcoming seventh album titled "Who We Used To Be," which was set to release on October 27, 2023. Alongside this announcement, Blunt released a single titled "Beside You" from the upcoming album, giving fans a taste of what to expect from this new musical chapter.

James Blunt's journey from his debut to his most recent album releases demonstrates his enduring passion for creating music that resonates with audiences worldwide. His ability to evolve while staying true to his unique style has solidified his place as a celebrated artist in the music industry.

# PERSONAL LIFE

James Blunt's personal life is a blend of various interests and connections.

He primarily resides on the picturesque Spanish island of Ibiza, where he finds inspiration and tranquility. Additionally, he owns a chalet in the charming Swiss Alpine village of Verbier, known for its stunning ski slopes. Blunt's association with the area is so strong that a ski lift in Verbier is named after him. In collaboration with motorcycle racer Carl Fogarty and rugby player Lawrence Dallaglio, he established a restaurant at the peak of the ski lift, aptly named La Vache, in 2012.

Blunt's personal life intersected with a significant legal matter when he became a victim of the News International phone hacking scandal. In response, he pursued a civil case and filed for damages related to the incident.

In terms of relationships, Blunt married Sofia Wellesley on September 6, 2014. Sofia Wellesley is the granddaughter of Valerian Wellesley, the 8th Duke of Wellington. The couple shares a family, with two sons. Notably, their elder son's godfather is fellow musician Ed Sheeran, and the godmother was the late Carrie Fisher, an iconic figure in the entertainment industry.

Recognizing his contributions to the world of music, James Blunt was awarded an honorary degree of Doctor of Music (Hon DMus) from the University of Bristol in 2016. This recognition further solidified his status as an accomplished artist.

Outside of his music career, Blunt is an active presence on social media, particularly Twitter, where he engages with his audience and showcases his self-deprecating sense of humor. His witty and relatable tweets have garnered him a following of over two million users. In 2020, his tweets were compiled into a book titled "How to Be a Complete and Utter Blunt: Diary of a Reluctant Social Media Sensation," published by Constable.

James Blunt's personal life is a rich tapestry of experiences, from his serene island residence to his cherished relationships and his engagement with fans through social media.

# CHARITY WORK

James Blunt's philanthropic endeavors showcase his dedication to various charitable causes and his commitment to making a positive impact.

Blunt is a patron of Help for Heroes, a notable charity focused on raising funds to enhance the quality of facilities and support available for wounded British servicemen. His involvement goes beyond just a title, as he has organized benefit concerts to raise funds for this cause, highlighting his heartfelt commitment to supporting those who have served their country.

His involvement with Médecins Sans Frontières (Doctors Without Borders) traces back to his time on operations in Kosovo. Blunt's encounters with this organization's humanitarian efforts deeply resonated with him. He has actively supported their cause by conducting meet-and-greet auctions at his concerts, allowing fans to contribute to this vital organization. He also took his support to another level by creating the documentary "Return to Kosovo," in which he revisited the people and places that left a mark on him during his time there.

Blunt's concerns extend to environmental causes as well. He utilized his platform to raise awareness about climate change by screening the trailer for "An Inconvenient Truth" at his concerts. He took a proactive step by incorporating an eco-friendly initiative into his concert ticket sales. For every advance ticket purchased through his designated website, a tree is planted, contributing to environmental conservation efforts.

His commitment to making a positive impact on the world was further demonstrated through his participation in the Live Earth concert at Wembley

Stadium in London on July 7, 2007. This global event aimed to raise awareness about environmental issues and inspire action.

Blunt's contributions were also felt in the realm of disaster relief. He lent his talents to the charity single "Everybody Hurts," which was released to support the 2010 Haiti earthquake appeal, showcasing his readiness to step in and help during times of crisis.

Through his active involvement with various charitable organizations, James Blunt has exemplified the power of using his influence and resources to make a meaningful difference in the lives of others and the world at large.

# DISCOGRAPHY

James Blunt's discography is a testament to his prolific musical career, spanning a range of albums that showcase his evolving style and artistry:

1. "Back to Bedlam" (2004): Blunt's debut album that catapulted him to international fame, featuring hits like "You're Beautiful" and "Goodbye My Lover."

2. "All the Lost Souls" (2007): His second album, which continued to showcase his emotive songwriting and musical depth, including tracks like "1973" and "Same Mistake."

3. "Some Kind of Trouble" (2010): A release that marked a slight shift in style, incorporating elements of pop and upbeat rhythms while retaining Blunt's signature emotional depth.

4. "Moon Landing" (2013): An album that saw Blunt return to his introspective and poignant sound, featuring songs like "Bonfire Heart" and "Postcards."

5. "The Afterlove" (2017): This album demonstrated Blunt's willingness to experiment with different sounds, incorporating electronic elements and collaborations, while retaining his heartfelt lyrics.

6. "Once Upon a Mind" (2019): Blunt's sixth album, continuing to explore his introspective themes with tracks like "Cold," showcasing his growth as an artist.

7. "Who We Used To Be" (2023): His upcoming seventh album set to release in October 2023, promising to bring new musical dimensions and introspection to his listeners.

James Blunt's discography reflects his evolution as an artist, from his early breakthrough with "Back to Bedlam" to his more recent explorations of different genres and themes. Each album contributes to the rich tapestry of his musical legacy, resonating with fans around the world.

Printed in Great Britain
by Amazon

40410493R00030